STRUGGLE OF A BLACK CHILD CONTINUES

AUTHOR: SINAKHOKONKE MAJOLA

THE STRUGGLE IS MY LIFE I WILL CONTINUE FIGHTING FOR BETTER DAYS" BY TATA NELSON MANDELA"

ISBN: 978-0-7961-7097-2(PRINT)

978-07961-7098-9(E-BOOK)

DICLAIMER

SINAKHOKONKE
MAJOLA

iF YOU BELIEVE IN YOUR SELF EVERYTHING IS POSSIBLE BL
CHILD
"ROME WASN'T BUILT IN ONE DAY WAIT FOR ME IM BUILDIN

I DEDICATE MY EFFORTS TO BUILD AND INSPIRE
EVERYONE. PEN DOWN YOUR THOUGHTS AND MANIFEST EVERYTHING YO
ABOUT ITS POSSIBLE BLACK CHILD

WRITTEN AND EDITED BY SINAKHOKONKE MAJOLA

3

PREFACE

Being black is who and what we are and we also proud of it, because we have overcome many obstacles we have faced as Africans.

Today I want to share with you'll in details what it was like being black and how It is like in our generation and also share the changing [Lifestyles of Our People].

I wrote this book to illustrate how life is twisting twirls nowadays and as someone good in environmental scanning.

I want to share my thoughts in a wider and broad extract about the black struggling and rich communities surrounding us, also how oppressed our people are even though we are so called a free South African country. I will also share alternatives to different aspects people face regarding things like financial freedom, changing their life style and many more. Stay tuned in.

I will also involve the political confluences that cause poverty and people to lose their jobs, poor service delivery and how politicians use us to play their dirty games.

I would like to introduce myself my name is Sinakhokonke Majola a born free. I was born in a small town called Escourt; I did my grade R and my grade 12 there.

I did my primary years in Ml sultan and my high school years in Drankensburg

Secondary School. What I really mean is that my life has been based there. In 2022 I started college in a town called Esikhawini under the city of Richard's bay. The college I embarked my studying journey at is called UMFOLOZI TVET COLLEGE, now it is 2024 my last year at college. Here am I with a beautiful thought of writing a treasuries book to build and heal a nation.

This is my first love in writing, my first self published book. I started writing it last year 2023. This year I decided to finish it since I have a mission to get my work all out there and my voice to be spread through meaningful words that will change lives.

I also have decided to write this book to express my creativity through writing since it has been a passion since I was in primary school.

I used to have a book where I used to write poems and lyrics of songs I would wish to release when I get recognition, since I had dreams of becoming an RNB or Hip Hop Artist.

I tried being a hip-hop artist but failed, eventually I opted 2021 out of that world and lost interest Due to the steepness of being an artist without enough support and exposure.
When you don't have enough resources, lack of funds and support you never make it big in the entertainment industry. How did I

really discover I can write a book? So since high school when it came to essay writing and writing speeches I always got nothing below 60 I was that good.

Not scared of performing, presenting in front of a crowd neither a class.

I am able to write an essay in a few minutes I'll be done. I have always been active when it came to written work or oral work, I love sharing ideas and solving issues. I also love to listen carefully when people speak or share different stories.

At college under a student command party called Team Sugar South African Students; 2023 last year I was appointed as a Deputy Secretary and also to contested the deputy secretary position during SRC elections. But eventually we lost.

I outdone my work perfectly when I was given a task it did not matter whether it was a deadline or not I was always willing to spread my wings.

I used to plan minutes of a meeting, speeches, and many more work related to secretarial work.

This made me ask myself; why not write a book while I have so much to share. So I have been conducting research on how to self publish a book since 2022.

Now it's my time to shine. This book is made for you black child. You are going to love it I am 100% sure you will enjoy every bit of it.

CONTENT

- CHAPTER 1- FREEDOM
- CHAPTER 2- LIFE IN THE TOWNSHIP/RURAL AREAS
- CHAPTER 3- DRUGS ARE KILLING THE FUTURE YOUNG MEN AND WOMEN.
- CHAPTER 4- INFLATION & POVERTY
- CHAPTER 5- PEER PRESSURE
- CHAPTER 6- EMPTY PROMISES
- CHAPTER 7 – RESPECT WILL PAVE YOUR WAY TO SUCCESS
- CHAPTER 8- STOP EXCUSES AND GET TO WORK

- CHAPTER 9-STOP BEING TOO MUCH COMFORTABLE
- CHAPTER 10- CREATING A SAFE ENVIRONMENT FOR OUR KIDS
- CHAPTER 11-RESPECTING YOURSELF AS A MEN OR WOMAN
- CHAPTER 12-PRIVELEGE OF POWER ON THE WRONG HANDS
- CHAPTER 13-FINANCIAL FREEDOM
- CHAPTER 14-FROM HERO TO ZERO
- CHAPTER 15-BLACK UNITY
- CHAPTER 16-INDEPENDENCE
- CHAPTER 17-THE BITTER SWEET TRUTH

- ## CONCLUSION AND ACKNOWLEDGEMENTS

'STRUGGLE OF A BLACK CHILD CONTINUES'

DON'T KILL YOURSELF TRYING TO RAISE THE DEAD

"MIKE TYSON"

FREEDOM

Our forefathers fought with the white monopoly to get this freedom we are misusing as the new generation. Some of them lost their lives through man slaughter by the so called South African invaders. Welcome to South Africa where you die for speaking the truth, you die for owning a profitable legitimate business.

We were never free from the beginning, a lot has been hidden in front of our 'own eyes'. We are so politically influenced we no more resolve things by talking.

'We Burn down Infrastructure', we Loot, we Break into government institutions without consulting with anyone's concern but that's the only way we get heard right! Rest in peace to all our ancestors who fought for our Behind bars freedom. We still uneasy and have heavy hearts but we have love for everyone, we forgive easily. We still believe in unity.

But that's Okay it's a Story for another Day .We were born to conquer every Circumstance. It's in our nature as long as we have a heart that beats; we will grow better in unity and solidarity. We are not cold as we are described I feel like we can do better.

Let's start practising what we preach good people, our constitution is rigged, how can a murderer run free in the streets? Oh! not enough evidence under section what, can 10 witnesses be wrong? I feel like we abusing powers.

Some laws suit certain individuals who have money to make cases go away. They pay lawyers and judges; doom the horrific case is over.
Some are in jail just because they only afford free lawyers that make them accept what they never done.

Not guilty until proven guilty is provoked, is that freedom when the law gives power to one individual?
They said freedom is coming we believed them, we still believe in them, isn't that insane?
Black child wake up there is no freedom you only get away with it when you generate wealth. Focus on money, your family and health. These people don't care about you, no ONE does.

LIFE IN THE TOWNSHIP/RURAL AREAS

Growing up in a Village or Township is not easy especially being raised by single mothers and fathers, some of us were raised by grannies and grandfathers.

Living in a township/village is very hard especially when there is no one working a paying job at home.

We grew up having to accept the home situation, sharing a meal in one plate. No wonder we love each other so much, we can relate to some of our struggles.
We come from humble beginnings, that's why we value our prestigious lives so much now.

Some of this poverty was brought to us since we were moved from big plots of land where government uses the land for their personal gain, to settlements where your neighbour is so close like your child next to you when sleeping on your bed.

We were moved to the so called RDP's our new settlements where 10 people in one family use one toilet, one kitchen, one small bathroom.

Right now if you can go to a local township school there is a child who went to school with an empty stomach, torn shoes, torn shirt and jersey.

His or her parents are no more or are poor to the extent that they do not even have a salary of R5900 per month.

But still that child has to go to school and conquer with the entire burden on top of his head. That child dear is likely to outshine all of them.

Pain makes us but pain can break us. Some children from poor households in South Africa leave school at a very young age mostly in grade 7 and 8.

This is due to the fact that there is no one working at home him or she has to try finding a job to change the home situation.

We were told we are going to have Shelter for all citizens after the apartheid era. But there is an estimate of more than a Million people who are Homeless & landless in South Africa. What Have we Become? My Government do you'll still have hearts or you'll using the power in your favour to deceive us. South Africa had no dangerous diseases during the times of the great King Shaka Zulu. Black people lived normal lives no one was on their neck, but look at what we have become since we were enslaved.

Is it normal that some families share one bed, toilet, kitchen, and dining room and also in some instances 10 family members share one shack? This system we are facing is wicked, to beat it completely is almost impossible, but we must keep trying we cannot continue to live like this it's unjust.

A white man I can't recall his name on this one interview told what he and his white colleagues had planned on getting rid of Africans through using fake vaccinations and Inflicting medication which causes diseases and rapidly kills my people. In some way I feel his statement was real.

Black people are suffering without a doubt, worse in their mother land.

In which he Said amongst those diseases they were injecting people with a drug that causes HIV and Aids which it Dominated and 'Killed Millions of Our People'. All this was done to get the 'Resources and

Mineral's Of Africa', it's Okay only God knows. Who are we to judge?

You can never kill a Horse by not making it drink water for two days. Luckily [HIV and Aids] cure was found and the spread of the virus has been minimised and people with [HIV and Aids] who use this medication tend to live a bit longer than expected.

This disease has left a lot of us with no parents sometimes with any living family members, it struck us a lot but we are doing better now.

My fellow people from the hood and gutters are struggling. They can't find proper jobs since some did not finish school; some are qualified but still can't find jobs. Most homes depend on Government **sassa** grants which offer money for children who have parents who are not working, elderly people at the age of 60 and above and also those with different disabilities. Also a new system for those who are not working from the age 18 has been put into action since covid 2019; it is called the SRD R350 GRANT.

People from the small townships and villages cannot access quality education even now it is still a huge problem.

There are many dropouts in our public schools each and every year; since parents struggle to participate most of the time due to financially being disabled from paying for their School fees, uniforms lunch, and children's transportation costs.

It is very hard to go to school with an uncomfortable uniform, torn clothes, torn shoes and going to school on an empty stomach.

You become the talk of the town; children tend to mock you since they do not understand your situation at home and what you personally go through every day.

This leads to the loss of love for school since you feel discouraged and children drop out with the hope of trying to find a job to enhance their lives and also provide their selves and provide at home.

Believe me these moments of seeing someone close to you go through this whilst there's nothing you can do to help them is totally nerve wrecking.

As someone who grew up in a Township I got to witness this as well, it's very hard to watch someone's live go down the drain but what can you do without the proper resources when you struggling too, absolutely nothing.

Even though I went to a diverse multi racial school I saw every struggle of what my family had to go through in order to pay for my school fee's, transport, Lunch& uniforms it was hard I won't lie but with god we prospered...God Said to us "No Odds set against us will prosper"

"I can be changed by what happens to me. But I refuse to be reduced by it".

"MAKE EVERY EFFORT TO CHANGE THINGS YOU DO NOT LIKE". IF YOU CANNOT MAKE A CHANGE, CHANGE THE WAY YOU HAVE BEEN THINKING YOU MIGHT FIND A NEW SOLUTION.

"ASK FOR WHAT YOU WANT AND BE PREPARED TO GET IT"

MAYA ANGELOU

DRUGS ARE KILLING THE FUTURE OF YOUNG MEN AND WOMEN

Drugs are becoming so popular to our society it's considered as a cool thing destroying your health and life nowadays.

We were once a Drug Free Nation, Who did this To Us? "Illegal immigrants, Foreigners, or our very Own People"

They all working together to kill a beautiful nation, South Africa has become a Pablo Escobar estate where drugs run in and out of the country like flies. Young boys and girls are living in the streets and also running away from their families because of these drugs.

I think there are many reasons our fellow brothers and sisters choose to take drugs. One of the reasons is to be accepted by society and fit in from your druggie friends they say when you smoke you are an [A LISTER] or Alpha Male which is crap because you killing your dreams.

The other reason is because of trying to avoid stressors or stress in the workplace, at home and 'All around the Environment'. Which may be stress from not getting a job, stress from losing parents, and stress from the hardships you facing in life?

This all leads to taking drugs without the thought that it is addictive, you just feel the ease on your head as you start it but as time goes on you feel A roaster or craving for smoking the harmful substances which are your likes of Dagga, heroin, alcohol, Cocaine, Cat and many more.

Drugs lead to serious consequences which can even claim one's life, people start bad habits like stealing from people, Raping woman, Dodging classes at school, Killing people and Ending up in jail, it also leads to losing a lot of people you love in a long-run process.

"Drug Addicts Cannot Control themselves" from stealing. When you start smoking dangerous drugs you are thrown out of home since you become a threat to your own family. No one trusts a man that can even steal from himself.

There is only one way to fix this drug problem we are facing right now as a country, but to defeat it we must be one. We need to bust down every 'Drug Lord' and confiscate the drugs and also jail these perpetrators to life imprisonment if it has to be that way. They are the ones who are killing the future of our youth. They also are constraining them to embitter their lives to be dependent on substances, while they get richer.

Starting drugs is a choice so is dumping them. A man that has entangled himself can free himself.

When I used to drink alcohol I was unstoppable I thought that was the best life.

No I was just lying to myself I wasn't
thinking straight.
If I gave my life to a bottle there wouldn't
be a book with my name ever written.

I found out that some of us especially
black people we don't need alcohol neither
drugs in our system that limits our
capabilities and strengths.

Sometimes you'll think just because you
have lost your job or not finding work you
have to give up and drink.
Maybe the bottle will calm you down and
you'll forget about reality.

The very next morning when there is no
alcohol in your system all those problems
you are running from come back.

32

Put the bottle down and face your fears,
face your reality, you need to think and
focus on the positives. Face the beast.

Focus on healing black child. Get out while
it's still early, consuming drugs limits your
true abilities.

INFLATION AND POVERTY

The hike of prices due to transportation costs which is caused by high Fuel prices, Lack of reliable electricity and infrastructure that can cater for everyone. This causes a lot of havoc on our economy at large.

As transportation costs increases businesses also increase their prices, which makes the lower earning people in South Africa suffer more and the rich to be richer. It hurts me everyday knowing there is a human being that has more than 100 billion but there are almost 712 million people who are facing poverty every single day. Crazy right!

Inflation leaves businesses with no choice but to dismiss some of their employees or retrench workers, since they have to also increase worker salaries when inflation hikes which doesn't happen most of the time.

This leads to the loss of jobs and job opportunities, making people not being able to provide for their children and themselves.

When people are unemployed they do all the wrong things and cross the line of the law to be able to provide food for their families. They get their selves involved in prostitution, selling drugs, robbing banks, house breaking, kidnapping and Est.

Most of the people I've seen who do crime
in the trenches it's because he/she wants
to be a provider at home, since in his or
her family all of them they are not working
they all depend on government grant money.

It's, just all about trying to change the
bad situation at home which is causing
futility and pain.
 Mothers rather starve themselves and give
their children the crumbs of food left;
then to watch their children sleep on an
empty stomach.

That's why they say a mother with courage,
love and dignity is strongest specimen alive.

Seeing People from the Outskirts of Town
Come to the Suburbs and Collect leftovers

and clothes from the dustbin will always be a trauma and a shock to me.

We call our country a Developing country that's haram, because 60% of South Africans are feeling the futility, suffering and pain of sleeping with an empty stomach, not being able to provide shelter for yourself and kids.

Since we are landless in our own motherland "ay" that's very demoralizing. Do you acknowledge the pain of going to school on an empty stomach, without proper shoes and clothes but with God if those children finish they become very successful in life.

There is a IsiZulu Saying which I'll say in English which says "In life you have to

suffer to reap great fruits for life".
Because even when you fall on your head
you cover it up and walk again and if you
have been on the floor a couple of times
you know the "whole vibe".

Unlike someone who was born wealthy and
misused their wealth and all of sudden
became broke. It becomes very hard for
them to accept the situation they facing
some even threaten their own existence by
committing suicide.

What I wanted to illustrate by this Whole
scenario is that when you feel pain too
much in life it becomes a norm, it becomes
a part of your body, spirit and mind.

So you must not be scared of circumstances you encounter just for a few moments and want it to stay with you for the rest of your life.

Wake up Black Child this land is still your home, fight for your motherland like how [King Shaka Zulu] did, fight with your heart and soul like 'Tata Mandela '.

Go to get information at school and be educated. Generate different sources of information to let you grow. Invest more on yourself more than anything, because they are worried about the same things that worry you.

Don't judge people by the way they portray themselves even painted portraits can look better than the person being painted.

I didn't write this book for chasing clout I want my fellow human beings part of the human race to be enlightened from the dark.

 I know we have a dark past but let's try to be in the light our future is looking hopeful if we unite the world will be our oyster.

We do not come from rich homes; we all have that poor background in us but through education, opening businesses of our own, building rental property and indulging ourselves into agriculture we will overcome poverty & nourishment. Also by learning how to invest in the stock markets we can change our lives rapidly. I have hope in my black people we will get through all of this lets trust our saviour god. I hope we will live to see the promise land.

 The black child will rise like the sun, Roar like a lion, spark like a falling shooting star. We have overcome hunger, death and slavery. This is just a walk in the park.

We will prevail. Today you may work for someone and they'll treat you badly just because they understand your financial status.

But trust me days are not the same my friend. Tomorrow might be a different day. There is an isiZulu saying that says "Namhlanje imina ksasa uwena "which means today is your turn, but tomorrow it will be mine.

Days are not the same. You will be fine my friend, manifest, persevere, pray and get to work it will happen.

 It doesn't matter where you come from look at me I wrote this book not even having a rand to my name. Money will come after. You have to manifest things before they truly come to true life existence.

 There is nothing wrong with having big dreams the biggest step is working towards those dreams and being disciplined. Without hardships there is no everlasting happiness, everything that you get without a good fight is short lived.

42

PEER PRESSURE

Peer pressure still hits my people harder than ever we describe ourselves as better than who, "I Dress better than who", I live in a bigger house than yours, my mother Is a doctor, I got more girlfriends than you, I am beautiful than who.

These are just a couple of the examples which we grew up under and they are still haunting us even till this day we want to be recognized by what we have and how educated we are.

 Instead of giving support to those who are unable to achieve those things and tell them all the tricks to become like how we got where we are, we do the opposite.

We ridicule, mock and discourage each other.

I think we have forgotten where we come from. We can't be happy seeing our brothers suffer there is no joke in seeing another child who has a mother that loves them suffer.

We shame them and make fun of our own sisters; whilst a brother can encourage and give out a reaching hand, why are we so heartless?

There is two types of pressure I will make mention of them.

First there is Positive pressure which is pressure of wanting to see yourself elevate in life do more, achieve more, explore the world, make dreams come true and collaborate with influential people with good deeds.

This is the best pressure one can put upon his or herself to attain all the things they wish to have in life and live a healthy life with no stress and worry or neither misery. Then we have our second type of pressure.

Negative peer pressure which is more of anticipating a character in which is more circled around what people think of you, wanting to impress someone by acting cool, looking gangster typical? This Pressure is not good for any human being because most decisions do not come from you it comes from pressure from the world.

Mostly they evolve around what you see and hear from people who you think are influential to you.

I've seen this happen a lot In school when cool kids form a group and start to do all the wrong things to be more appealing and relevant than other children.

They tend to make the other children a joke because of their differences when compared to them you only become "dope" when you try to belong and be like how they are imitating someone's Character never last. Because that's not really who you are ,that's just a Character so you have to love who you are and embrace being alive on this beautiful earth 'some Left too soon', 'some never made it.

You need to create your own empire and explore you, if you don't do that your success will be constrained.

Don't try to be like someone because there is no one on this earth better than you. Pressure is just a state of mind that can be handled please try to handle it. At primary and at Secondary School I Used to be friends with the unpopular kids not that I wasn't Cool and known in School, I was cool but there was something different with the un-cool kids that made me want to learn something from them. They don't just mock each other the whole day and compete or talk about girls they talked business, furthering their studies, buying beautiful cars and getting married.

Also things like the bad weather conditions affecting the country, big dreams after finishing high school, what they want to see themselves become in a space of 5 years. So it was more about literacy and talking about reality events and million dollar dreams.

I have a saying I always tell people around me whenever they feel down the un-coolest things are the coolest things.

If you don't belong don't stress something's are just not for you. Be Kind and be yourself and have a purpose in life.

Most of us got involved in wrong doings because we wanted to please our families and friends of which they don't even care much.

Some say when you are pressured into narcotic substances or alcohol there is no way back you only come in and the door gets shut , I say that's pure lies that's all in the state of mind.

You can change for you, yourself, and family don't let the haters win.

My fellow black brothers and sisters are misled by family and friends I mean how does a parent let you in the house with stolen goods.

Oh no! who am I to ask that, it's poverty that made us this pro-typical animal beings, evil people who no more know what the purpose of life is.

Never let someone get in your head dear. Remember when you suffer the consequences of any problem you get in trouble alone and no one saves you. It's better to suffer consequences at your expense than to suffer at someone's expense. Just imagine the pain having to pay dues for something you cannot account for. Be wise my friend "when days are dark friends are few".

EMPTY PROMISES

As a South African black citizen born and bred in the motherland of kings and queens. I have been promised a land that is not conquered by armies and solidified by displacing my people.

I am hope for a better tomorrow, hope for my parents. I was promised free education, free housing, free water, and a peaceful South Africa.

Since 1994 South Africa has not been the same, we living in a new era now we are born free but yet again born in an era full of deception and lies.

We were promised big things but some of those promises that were promised to my mother are now being promised to me.

We are young educated youngsters struggling to find jobs, since politicians have us on the palm of hand.

Nepotism is ruling the world it's a matter of who you know not what you know. When it comes to it our qualifications they have become worthless.
They hire incompetent people only to find out the outcome of doing that leads to numerous breakdowns and accidents that constraints the growth of our economy.

Wake up my people when I talk about my people I'm talking about the human race whether black, brown, white we all come from 1 god we share one blood. I Think I'm the last person to be promised something and wait on it for a long time.

This is because most of those things we wait long time from our government are just worthless. We must act with immediate effect and encounter all these counterfeits we are facing.

Mr Mandela's Years in prison seem to be wasted, my people are getting out of hand nowadays each day more than 71 people are murdered in South Africa is that freedom, more than 60% of women in South Africa experience rape and assault.
Is this what we really voted for, is this the freedom our fore-fathers fought for."OOoh" I think right now they are turning in their graves.

Now what I don't understand more is that our black successful brothers, our own delegates, ministers, presidents, government workers and many more in higher positions are the most corrupt people you've ever knew. By the way those are the same people leading our country to the end of a dark tunnel.

Those are the people we trust with all our lives. Ey' it's a pity that we have such short minded leaders who don't have the balls to lead without discrimination and consider, listen and acknowledge the problems that our fellow citizens are facing.

One day whether you rich or poor just sit on the municipal benches in your town or in the city parks and observe at our hopeless society.

Young girls who aren't even women yet getting dropped by Old men Via their cars or SUV's manipulating the girls for sex and giving them money in exchange, since they are so desperate they have to provide at home with that money. We must protect our children by all means possible, this cannot go on someone has to stop it.

Men are smoking drugs on the streets, the homeless don't even know where to go since their family members either rejected them or they don't even know a place called home. Sad neh?

Observing society breaks my heart every day but every day I get a lesson from the streets. Be humble the streets are cold out there,

I see small change in our country we still have a long way to go. A lot has to be changed and a lot of us need to change our mindset, so we can all move towards the same evolving direction.

We still in the dark we were promised lights."Hope is able to see that there is light despite the darkness".

We pray for better leaders in the world who are morally upright, well spoken with respect, dignity and a lot of kindness with god anything is highly possible.

RESPECT WILL PAVE YOUR WAY TO SUCCESS

Respect is what we give, what we owe and a way to express love.

You don't have to respect people because of their title black child it doesn't matter whether a person is a hobo, a doctor, police and many more. Respect has nothing to do with what job title people hold.

It's all about being morally upright and acknowledging someone's presence.

"To the living we owe Respect and to the dead we owe only truth".

57

Respect on its own shows what type of character a person is and it makes it easy for a people to communicate with each other, since they share the same type of energy.

But before earning respect from others you should first respect yourself first and only by then you will compel others to respect.

Respect is very important in building a solid relationship whether a "lovey dovey" relationship or friendship amongst peers.

As a Zulu man I was taught respect at a very young age there is a saying in isiZulu which says for a tree to bear fruits some of its branches must be cut of so that it can grow again into a tree that bears beautiful and juicy fruits.

Success needs you to leave comfort, no one wins when they are comfortable. Remember you are your biggest opponent. No one can beat you. You are your greatest aspiration.

A child needs to be taught respect at a very young age before reaching womanhood or manhood.

I was taught not to call elders by their Name I call a man "Baba" and a woman "Mama" doesn't matter whether they are my family or not, but that's how you show respect in my culture. But as times change young people are losing their morals bit by bit.

In most cases I blame some of their parents how can you drink alcohol, go to party and smoke in front of your child what example are you showing the child?

After that when they become like how you are, you blame them isn't this a family thing and you paved the way!

Where I come from even when people are kissing on Television when watching with elders you had to look away and act as if you can't see. But nowadays young children have Smartphone's with Face book, Twitter, Instagram and Tiktok which Promote explicit content with sex tapes and all the nonsense around the world you can think about. They know these things more than us.

I think we are in a sink hole we losing it bit by bit. It can be fixed I think some of the old cultural ways of our culture should be kept constant to leave in a peaceful respectful environment

But how is that possible when women dress like they at a pool party everyday exposing their bodies. Who am I to judge everyone has identity issues these days, we want to belong.

Oh mighty lord I fear for the children yet to come we have totally lost it. Let's respect our bodies, let's respect women as men and women must also respect men. When we are one, we will conquer the world. Love lasts when it is shared equally.

STOP EXCUSES AND GET TO WORK

As black people our upbringing as we grow is very tough. So we tend to make that hard upbringing something to always make an excuse about when we face difficulties, or when we don't make it in life. Stop feeling sorry for yourself get to work.

I've seen many people in my lifetime saying words like if I grew up with rich parents maybe I could have been something in life, this probably just shows me how much my people have lost hope in themselves.

Not to be rude but saying what if? Won't pay for the bills, neither take your children to school.

So we need to teach the young generation to know how to move on and not to be stuck in the past, simply because sometimes when focusing more on our negative past we tend to demoralize our abilities and lose faith in our dreams.

The world is meaningful to those who are able to forgive themselves about their passive mistakes. Remember even a child doesn't just start to walk out of the blue, it starts crawling, falls, stands up & falls on its head and cry's but still stand up and try's to walk again. They do this cycle until they can walk properly.

After that a beautiful smile starts blooming on their faces.

Basically what I wanted to illustrate or say to someone who has been through a lot they must forget about who there used to be and focus on what and who they have become.

Embrace and love their selves, because we only have one chance to be happy in life so we must stop dwelling in the past.

No one will save you black child you have been on your own since you were born, family can't save you look you couldn't even save yourself.

Exhaust all the skills, all the resources you have to achieve your goal. It's not always greener on the other side but its better being on the other side.

Poverty cannot stop us we all grew up in mud houses so what? is that your excuse, get over it. This year they will know you black child.

Try listening to the interviews of rich people you will get to hear the struggles they undergone to reach where they are. Nothing falls from the trees like fruits for free in this life the price of progress is pain.

"Be water my friend"

'Bruce lee'

STOP BEING TOO MUCH COMFORTABLE

Being too comfortable because you still have parents to rely on while you have finished school it's useless.

I don't recommend someone who can see the difference between right and wrong and can think for him/her self to be comfortable. If you do not have a reliable source of income, which is not from parent's allowance, you must try by all means to work on something and thru your hustle & hard work your shall strive for a better life.
That's my kind of people. The game changers, who do the unthinkable and still come out alive without a stretch,

Being reliant on someone is not good simply, because a person is like a risky business he or she may shut down at any moment.
Trust your own abilities you are more than capable.

We have to work hard and change our homes while our families are still alive and reward the support system which carried us from infantry to adulthood, giving us a meal every day of which I will truly forever be grateful for.

Now it is the time to give back, now it is time to make our loved ones happy and not saying these unrealistic poor statements like saying giving back or providing our parents with home necessities is forced black tax.

Only people who cannot think out of the box say these sentimental things. Giving back to your creators is considered as blessings from God himself in my Zulu tribe. Giving back has many benefits it all starts at home with giving back to parents by buying groceries at home when working in return you earn their respect get their blessings.

Giving back to your family and community when you are working is such a beautiful thing we must get used to it. It doesn't need names because it's part of who we are, so it is more of securing our roots.

If you grew up with both parents until you matriculated you must be very grateful, most of us grew up with one or no parents. There is only one term that makes sense to us "The art of hustling".

When you don't have someone to cry on, you are left with no choice but to raid the streets or find a job that can pay any amount of money that will make you have a meal to sleep eat before you sleep.

At this aspect you have to go hustle, because you only hardly driven by hunger & everything doesn't seem meaningful to you. True power lies in hunger.

Find your true abilities. This makes one be able to survive all shades thrown towards them and to keep on being on survival mode.

You are lucky you still have a roof on your head. While others are sleeping in pipes and in the cold streets there's the lucky you who gets a meal everyday and good quality free education. Think about the chance you are given and be considerate about those that sleep with an empty stomach every single day. Is it fair?

You should be grateful that God gave you the life that you have.

Don't ever think god has walked away or abandoned you the biggest blessings take time.

 Utilize your education and hustle hard to make a meaningful contribution to those who do not have anything. Help those in need you shall be blessed.

Try to be kind when you become successful, try giving back to your community by offering clothes, food, rehabilitation for those who are involved in drug use, donate food to old ages and many more.

Be different from the world, look at life upside down from another perspective don't give up on your black brothers and sisters.

Everyone deserves a second chance when I say black child I am not talking about my fellow brothers and sisters only, I'm mentioning everyone who is an African with a heart and who wants to do better.

Let us work hard and prosper all our dreams we cannot live our lives like we in some sort of cartoon or Disneyland show. Last but not least let's stop staying in a comfort zone while life isn't comfortable.

The world is meaningful to those who have a purpose on making contributions to change their lives.

CREATING A SAFE ENVIRONMENT FOR OUR KIDS

How do we go about creating a safe space where our kids grow up to be what we wanted them to be, successful? I guess. It is highly impossible to predict the future. But you can secure the future of a child by trying by all means to support their talents; all the stars you see on screen were once dreamers.

A child is a blessing from disguise no matter the disability after all no child is born with all gifts embrace what god gave you. Providing small resources to our children especially the black community encourages our kids, those memories last forever.

I remember a time when I was in primary I asked my mother to buy for me soccer boots. She bought them the following day. Moral of the story small things build character and matter most.

Behind every successful child there is a parent no matter if that parent is their bloodline parent or not. As long as a child is a child, that child is yours. I will never leave an innocent soul in the bus stop hanging just like that never.

I want to engage with him or her ask her what happened, did the transport leave without her. If we become responsible nothing can break us. I want our kids to have a far better life even better than the one we had. I won't lie I was raised by a village. South Africans still have hearts there's some good in us. Let's carry on that way. I have met all races as I went to multi racial schools and had experience of growing up in multiple communities. We tend to work much better together.

A child must be taught to love everyone no matter the skin colour. Racism must be a thing of the past. We cannot fight over something we do not understand. No child is born racist neither xenophobic they adopt those habits from home or from people close to them. So as the generation Z parents born in democratic South Africa we cannot dwell in the past we have our own history to create.

Children must be protected from drugs and unprotected sex. How do we contain that? We keep them busy all time and instil discipline in them. We must stop over spoiling them and give them money or buy them gifts when they are demanding things.

A child is a child after all. We need to start having chats about what is concerning them before they end up doing drugs because of stress and anxiety.

Church too is a good place for our children they need to grow up knowing god. He who knows god will be saved even when he has sinned.

I so wish other races adopted the Zulu REED dance culture of girls who are virgins to go to camps with their god mothers to groom them and advice them about how to prevent being caught up in a situation where you find one having 2 children at the age of 19 years. I don't judge that child.

We are human after all. If that child had someone who had a role to play that child could have been in a greater space.

Most of these disastrous events occur mostly in the negligence of parents mostly in black households where you find parents fight in front of children, do drugs in front of children.

Remember you are your children's biggest super star. Once you create a negative image in your child's head that leads to serious consequence, where you find a child bullying other students at school or around the neighbourhood.

They learnt that at home did they? So we must protect these kids from all these scenarios. Someone must intervene you cannot say as long as that is not my child I am not involved.

Are you really human? When you are able to see and read between the lines of wrong and right you will be a good parent, a good citizen.

Your neighbour's child cannot starve in your presence knowing well you have something you can offer. If you don't feel any sympathy for kids find god.

Most of us as black children in the townships or in rural areas find ourselves in drugs because of absent parents.

You may find one needed someone in his/her life to play a mother or father figure in their live to be a good child or do good deeds.

Save that child! God will bless you. You may find that by helping, advising that child you have saved their lives from the ruthless streets. Let's help these vulnerable souls.

Men and women never let anything bad happen to that child in your presence. The black child must succeed "SEKUYI'SKHATHI".

The biggest disease that pains me every day is parents who tend to see girlfriends in their child that is pure evil. I blame the usage of substances like alcohol and drugs.

But how can I blame drugs when a man of god takes advantage of a child, an aunt takes advantage of her niece. We are ill god must intervene.

Who can we trust with our children the uncles ill, the mothers wicked the father is a scavenger.

I think we have totally lost it. What type of father grows a child to a women or men and end up raping them? That's sick as hell.

Black child wake up protect that child. My child exposes that devil we will protect you.

I wonder what the law, who is the law, is, because I feel the law only grooms criminals. We are failing these kids. We are a mess, we need to take action, and we need therapy.

Stop using these children for fighting your relationship battles. The poor child cannot even function in school.

Mommy told the child to say daddy raped her. While she just wanted to make him feel pain. That creates pain to all corners.

The father loses his life and kids; the chid loses a chance to grow up with a present father figure.

Just because you wanted one person to feel pain you have cause ocean tears to the world. Stop using children for personal gain.

We cannot control our children's feelings but we can teach them how to navigate them by how we navigate our own.

And in doing so, we can better provide a safe, supportive environment for them to grow

RESPECTING YOURSELF AS A MAN OR WOMEN

Why should you respect yourself dear black child? You are someone's inspiration. You are joy.

You are light in the dark, a remarkable specimen. Brought up in roots where respect is the foundation of building a home.

We are raised very well by parents most of us. Even if you don't have a parent, in Kwa-Zulu Natal every mother is a mother of the nation, every father too is a father of the nation.

A child raised by a village has great values. You had great values, what changed my brother, what changed dear sister.

We are so full of our self we don't even want to help that granny to carry her groceries to her house like how we used to do.

That's where our blessings lie. Have you forgotten, have you forgotten about the beautiful hills back home. You promised your parents after finishing varsity, after getting a job you will build them a beautiful house.

A good environment never changes one but reminds him of where they come from. Sometimes you just got to go home things aren't making sense? go home.

Do you think your kids will want to grow up to be like you? Are you a super hero or a super zero? Change, change for your kids. Stop embarrassing yourself.

Entertainment never ends. Pursue something, do something. When your brain gets busy the right way things come your way.

Do you think your son or daughter admires that dress code? Revealing isn't it. One day you will be a father, one day you are going to be a mother.

Would you rather   be loved or feared. Change that attitude get back to that inner child you used to be, very humble, very respectful.

Respecting yourself increases your value as a person for example when I used to drink no one saw my potential they just saw a young men who has lost hope shattering his dreams through alcohol.

 Now I'm at my best, sober as a judge every decision I make is superb.

My mind is on a doing better than yesterday mode I do worry about money every day.

 But I worry because I want to create something with that certain amount.

I no more want to be seen alcohol happy or make people who don't care about me happy with my money.

The following day I'm broke again. What kind of husband or father will I be?

My point is respecting yourself makes everyone inspired by you. Your words become wisdom.

Everyone wants to associate with you. You become an asset to the community. Your family feels safe around you.

They treasure and admire you, isn't that wonderful.

Who doesn't want to be loved by their family? When you respect yourself you become responsible.

Respect yourself; you'll be given the same respect you give to others including yourself.

Value yourself black child they don't like seeing you become a precious pearl.

PREVELEGE OF POWER WHEN GIVEN TO THE WRONG HANDS

When power lands in the wrong hands we are likely to suffer the consequences of one man. They were once good people with sympathy and remorse the world changed them can't blame some of them much.

Its better dying and leaving a legacy than to leave history, history won't feed your family black child. But keep your things legit get the move correctly.

When you are in power being accountable for your actions is important. No one must control you with money you calling the shots already you don't need power you are in power already.

No man wants to be controlled like a TV. When someone says jump you say how high like our politicians.

Just look at the decisions some make you can see there is someone behind them for what reason will I disembark my rules, my ethics for greed, for money, for power.

What is power without having the authority to say a word? Are you a lion, are you a tigress, nah! Seems like you've lost your womanhood, seems like you've lost your manhood.

Are you going to let them control you black child? No one has authority over your life only god is. When power and authority falls on dirty hands everything goes south.

It corrupts one who is power hungry to lead a nation with ill intentions, knowing well their intention is to use the position for self praise, self accomplishment and self gain.

He who forgets where they come from and forgets about their family will fall and lose everything they have.

Because when we are uplifted we are given a chance to change our communities and change lives of lost souls of young people.

When you abort a mission but you already in the battle ground you may suffer the consequences.

It is very hard to build but everything can be destroyed in a very few seconds. When they try to involve you in these shady deals black child think about the future of your family, think about your children, and are you willing to lose all that just because of greed.

Don't do it black child if god wants you to be the new Elon Musk he will make you one. Our biggest problem is Ego we want to be better than each other.

We don't want to be better ourselves. You are your best competitor no one can beat you when you compete with inner child instilled in you.

The strongest person is the one who controls their senses and is not controlled by their senses.

Such person can put restraints over themselves and do not give in into anger, hatred, jealousy, greed, temptation, pain, pleasure or narcissism.

They can sacrifice even the dearest thing for them for the sake of righteousness or good deeds.

As leaders of the community if we can change this system of deception and lies, a nation of opulence, progress and peace can be created. We are part of the problem.

No man was born a gangster; it haunts him and if it finds him weak he dares the day it found him. We shall suffer the consequence of our wrong doings.

Everything that happens in the dark will be revealed in light one day. Don't enslave yourself we were once forced remember now no one controls us now. We are in charge. Africa will be great again.

"Anyone entrusted with power will abuse it if not also animated with the love of truth and virtue, no matter he be neither a prince nor one of the people"

FINANCIAL FREEDOM

How do we go about being financially free as black people? Good question hey! The first step of being financially free is stopping relying on the government, on someone to dictate how much we are worth and how much we must earn.

When you are in control of your finances you are able to make decisions and choices based on your desires and goals. Rather than being limited by how much things cost. We need to start investing in our future rather than killing it.

We are abusing the fun. That leads to our future being a joke and very funny to our enemies.

You want to be a mocking bird? If not get to work loosen your mind think like a pro.

Stop saying why not me, act. Do you ever think about who created that expensive bottle of Hennessey you treasure so much, do you ever think how they turned an idea to a product. You need to chance.

Ask yourself questions black child do research you will find answers to your question. No one just woke up with a company, not unless they inherit it. You build it from stretch.

You do not get profitable the first few years, you constantly grow with it and understand the difficulties of running it and the positive & negative outcomes of your business space.

Why am I imposing this to an employee mindset, sorry to abuse your working mind but the reality is that every black child has to have several streams of income to survive. You cannot depend on a job, what if they fire you? Are you going to wait for another miserable 2years looking for a job? Really are serious. Shift that mindset black child no one is going to save you if you become useless to them you cannot be used anymore. But your business will never say you are useless, your hustling grind will never neglect you.

It's okay losing it all rock bottom is beautiful, the struggle of rising has beautiful stories when you on the other side.

We cannot keep on creating other peoples empire black child it is enough. Let's find financial education because it cannot find us. You have to dig for it, read books about it.

Study rich people how they get money forget about your government that has the same promises since Jesus left earth, even when he returns they'll still promise you a better tomorrow. There is no tomorrow. You are the dictator of how your tomorrow will be; you have the power and authority to land yourself in the riches.

First step is to forget and forgive the fact that someone who is human like me and you are going to get you out of your current financial status.

They only care about people close to them you are just their ladder to success black child resist it. You deserve the world why not you?

Escape the matrix now or never. The only way to change your current situation is to start implementing. As I am writing this book I don't even have money to publish it yet, but I am taking action.

 If you believe in something so bad it is possible no one can stop you. If your desire is burning no one can stop that fire in you. Stop thinking you need first to start something. You need to read more first, conduct thorough research while waiting for your time. When money comes to someone who already has good investment plans about that money, they turn to be unstoppable when it comes to generating wealth.

Why so? They have studied the environment they understand what they are dealing with. What losses they may endure during the process and what they willing to lose or do in order to change that situation. Money needs you to practise, be aware of economic change happening not I your country only but around the world. We you seek financial freedom you have to watch as much news as possible to understand the economical pro and cons of the business nature, what controls what, what drives prices up and down, what conflict or war does to a certain business sphere. Most of these things are often mentioned in school text book but not in context that's why we tend to ignore them because once you know about how an economy functions and all the business factors. Your mind ultimately will have another perception of the world at large, you will understand investing easily.

They are keeping all this away from you black child. They don't want you to be successful they want you to worry about being educated and brag about your degrees, matriculation certificates amongst each other.

While their children; leave school from grade 10, we work for those guys the uneducated champ.

While we were solving X and Y they were hustling their way up to create nothing to something. And there's us we have consumed maybe more than 50 books in our brains but we thinking about being hired we don't think about creating.

Wake up black child. Our mothers and fathers wanted a better life for us when they took us to school.

 Let's start using the knowledge we gathered from Colleges and Universities in our communities or surroundings while we wait for our dream jobs.

If we can use education to create we will become unstoppable. Look at how china is so advanced. Why is so?

They use education to transform the environment and the world. They see opportunities they produce new ideas every now and then.

Don't you have ideas dear sister, don't you have visions brother? You do right oh you are scared of who is going to support you. If something makes remarkable sense they will be convinced.

The product will sell like sweets, if it doesn't at first glance don't quit. Keep going no matter how steep is the road.

If you want to be financially free you cannot procrastinate, be resilient at all costs. Financial freedom comes with a lot of sacrifices.

It is like trying to change this one bad person to turn into a good person, very hard right?

Beggars are losers and winners are choosers.

You have two choices its either you become a king or a king's servant.

Start knowing the difference between assets and liabilities.

You cannot own a car for R1 million when your bank does not have that kind of money unless that car can make back that money in a short term space.

Assets are our insurance during times of uncertainties that can happen. You can still take care of your family.

Owning property, companies, real estate, fleet that generates money, farms and more makes us financially free.

When you let money work for you become totally free from financial stressors.

You must also have other digital investments like insurance, investment in stocks, bank investments to avoid being caught up with being sent back to rock bottom.

It is very tough to rise when you fell from the peak of a mountain.

Invest 40% of what you earn on assets, on your business, on your stock investments you will not regret it black child.

Go and start reading differently you will escape the matrix very soon.

If you want to learn more about financial freedom go read Robert Kiyosaki's book called "RICH DAD POOR KID" I promise you blood you will certainly be relieved from financial slavery after reading it.

ECCLESIASTES 11: 2

"INVEST YOUR MONEY IN SEVEN VENTURES, YES, IN EIGHT, YOU DO NOT KNOW WHAT DISASTERS MAY COME UPON THE LAND."

FROM HERO TO ZERO

In this life you can fall my fellow brothers and sisters. Power can be taken whether you doing good or bad. You can lose it all.

All your efforts gone to waste just like that. Welcome to the real world.

It is very hard to suffer when you have never suffered, I understand brother but your situation right now will fade like that heartbreak you endured remember. It happens, its life cousin.

From the "Burbs" to a life with no hope where you just waiting for your break-through or you just waiting for your final day, Very brutal if you think about it.

You were once hailed and praised like a king. Those that used to be your friends have changed upon you. Don't be sorry for yourself you did nothing wrong champ life happens sometimes. Pick yourself up you can still rebuild it all black child.

Your fame and fortune has vanished and has been replaced by shame and disgraces don't worry a bit we all make mistakes sometimes.

 They pity for you some are even disgusted when they see you mind you, some of them are where you are because of you and are not returning the favour now.

 Remember we said to ourselves we do not help people for benefits we do it from the heart to get that feeling of pleasure, we do I for god.

When you helped them it was free will if they forget you they forget but your lord will never forget you.

Try again he will support you, no one cares you gave your money to charity or you used to help the church financially.

When the tap to drink is closed they run away from you, who would want to be friends with a bum. At least you have learnt your lesson.

Only trust a rock since it cannot move neither speak it's always in one position.

People change like seasons once they have what they want they move on. Look at failure as a test even hero's have their ups and downs.

We take our time to build but it can shrink within a short period of space, we came here on earth naked my friend we will leave everything here.

So there's nothing to lose we just being played by the Matrix the only thing that's valuable is that precious breath.

The wealth we create is for us to survive on this earth, be happy with our friends and family but when you think of it in a clear mindset there is no value in all these fancy things we own. Human life is the real treasure and value. As a leader of your family, a mother, father, brother, sister no one can take that from you rather than god.

When you become like water and just go with the flow of the environment you don't think of any situations, you are able to adapt no matter how tough the situation is.

You must patch your wounds and pull your chin forward, no one can stop you black child not even the sea. You have seen it all.

Activate the inner child again that wants to see his or self in a better environment, in a better car, in a better country.

It is all possible you can still make it no matter the age you are in right now.

Look at some women they give birth when they are 50 years which is a miracle, some men and women get their Degrees at 60 this clearly symbolises that an old age to achieve something does not exist.

You will get what you want when the time comes you have to meet it halfway by putting enormous effort.

Now wake up the burning beast in your burning desire and go claim your crown mate.

They will talk a beautiful story about you black child, the men or women who fell on the Ground from the peak of a valley and arose "FROM HERO TO ZERO" but never gave up and put himself back on track, back to his real throne "Bathathe" CHAMP! FROM ZERO TO HERO they will call you royalty black child.

It is not a matter of how you fell but what describes your true power is how you took a stand from a place with no hope, no joy neither love.

All you could here is voices speaking through your ears saying if I could have done this and that maybe! You conquered the voices still, you conquered the haters, and you conquered the evil woes spread about you. Ooh what a warrior you are brother. Giving up is not a solution it's a disease instead put up a good fight you will prevail dear sister. I hope you truly win.

BLACK UNITY

Can we really unite? Is it possible, do you ever think it will happen anytime soon? Why do you think so? If we are divided we give an enemy a clue, we give them ideas how to attack us.

Are you mad for being called dumb? Are you dumb! I don't think so. We need to fix ourselves stitch those wounds black child.

I know healing is a process but we family after all if we let them separate us. We will never have any family gatherings anymore? Our kids will not witness the beauty of being around different beautiful creations & different souls. They won't even share a beautiful moment and rejoice the day of family!

I understand black child our family tree was dismantled and packed on a boat long ago. Let's not lose the crumbs left, if we work together the family tree of our kids might be restored and turned into generational history.

Look at me and yourself we don't even know the closest people in the family tree, our grandfathers and fathers. Do you think these children will survive like how we surviving?

I don't think so. So wish I had a team called family, very rare to find isn't it. How will we achieve opulence and wealth without a proper team, highly possible but to reach greater heights you need black authority, you need black unity, and you need family.

Behind every successful man there is a team called family.

People who are there and will be there for you like a wife who truly meant what she vowed on her wedding date "through thick and thin "that's the winning team.

We need loyal people to generate wealth who will uplift us in pain uplift us in our successful moments cherish our efforts.

So my question is to you the one black child? Do you think you'll manage? Why not support your sister, why not support the movement created by your family to move from rags to riches.

I think if we can rise together we can be respected like the OPPEINHEIMERS.

Just imagine because those people made money in a shady way and we are going to move responsible and ethical.

Won't that motivate a black child? Look at people like Pablo Escobar he had a team on his side till the very last day of his evil deeds.

Why not have a team and win in an ethical righteous manner; when working with a team can be used for bad doings and still come right.

We must not make the Devil happy.

Stop thinking you better than your sister. Be better than you, compete with you. Be an inspiration to your brother.

Take total authority of the situation you in, change for the better. You are dynamite indeed. No one is like you and there will never be another you. Sometimes from the bitterest experiences comes an awakening. Focus on your dreams black child.

INDEPENDENCE

What is independence? I think it is being able to manage yourself financially, emotionally and health wise. Knowing what is good and not good for you. Independence comes from taking responsibility of your life and standing alone.

You cannot say you are independent under your families roof, you cannot say you are independent in a rental house. What if you cannot afford rent? You'll ask for help from family isn't?

To be totally independent takes time and various risks; so you have to commit in order to be a provider at home and in your community through numerous things like studying for years after studying starting a business or seek for a well paying job.

Independence is a crucial aspect of personal growth and development, empowering an individual to forge their own paths and shape their destinies.

"The best way to find your self is to lose yourself in the service of others."

Mahatma Ghandi

This quote emphasizes the significance of giving back and contributing to society, which helps individuals to discover their purpose and develop a sense of self reliance.

By being of service to others, one learns the true value of independence and the importance of using it for the greater good.

Independence is not about the autonomy but also about being personally responsible. "Man is condemned to be free; because once thrown into the world, he is responsible for everything he does."With independence comes the need to take ownership of one's actions and the consequences they may bring. This quote serves as a reminder that freedom is not only a privilege but also a responsibility.

To conclude the concept of independence encompasses self reliance, autonomy, and personal responsibility.

By examining the insights provided by influential figures, it becomes evident that independence is essential for personal growth and development.

As we embrace the path less travelled and face life challenges with courage and resilience, we can unlock the power of independence and create lives filled with purpose and meaning. Seek for independence black child.

.THE BITTER SWEET TRUTH

No one cares about you black child you are on your own. We are facing an ongoing bitter system that wants to keep us poor.

The lives of black people, both historically and in contemporary society, are characterized by a complex and nuanced reality that encompasses both triumph and struggle.

It is also important to acknowledge the progress made in racial equity, also it's crucial to recognize the ongoing challenges we are facing as black communities on a daily basis.

Throughout history as black people we have faced numerous systemic discrimination, violence, and oppression, which have significantly impacted our opportunities and life outcomes.

The legacy of slavery, segregation, and racial injustice continues to reverberate today, with issues such as police brutality, mass incarceration, economic inequality, and health disparities disproportionally impacting black communities.

Despite these challenges, black people have made significant contributions to society in various fields, including art, science, music, politics and civil rights activism.

Our resilience and perseverance in the face of adversity have inspired many and contributed to social progress.

It's very important to acknowledge the progress made in addressing racial inequalities, such as the election of the first black President in South Africa our very own "Tata Nelson Mandela", but also to recognize that much work remains to be done to achieve true equality and justice for black people worldwide.

You have encountered many defeats black child but you cannot be defeated. Rise above all odds set against you

ISSAIH 60:20

"Thy sun shall no more go down; neither shall thy moon withdraw itself: for the lord shall be thine everlasting light, and the days of thy morning shall be ended"

CONCLUSION & ACKNOWLEDGEMENTS

First and foremost, I would like to express my heartfelt gratitude to my family, who have been the constant source of love, encouragement, and support throughout my writing journey and career.

Their unwavering belief in me has the foundation upon which this book was built.

To my friends, family and children, I hope this copy fills your cup of tea with love and joy.

I would also like to acknowledge myself since I have been instrumental in writing and also editing this book on my own.

Finally to my readers without you this book would not exist.

My enthusiasm for storytelling and my willingness to embark on this journey alone and still make it possible is what makes the world of literature so magical. Thank you for allowing me to share my world with you.

With deepest gratitude and appreciation,

SINAKHOKONKE MAJOLA

"ROME WASN'T BUILT IN ONEDAY WAIT FOR ME I AM BUILDING UP"

INACOZZZI TRADING PTY LTD

Contact details for insights about the book also to fast tracking my writing journey and personal life and business.

I might also share how to publish your own book as an upcoming writer 'chow'

Instagram: SINAKHOKONKEMARJOLAR

Face book: SINAKHOKONKEMARJOLAR

YOUTUBE: SINAKHOKONKEMARJOLAR

TIKTOK   : SINAKHOKONKEMARJOLAR

TWITTER   : SINAKHOKONKEMARJOLAR

EMAIL   sinakhokonkenacozzzi@gmail.com

Business Whatsapp: 0729134520

www.ingramcontent.com/pod-product-compliance
Lightning Source LLC
Chambersburg PA
CBHW060523030426
42337CB00015B/1975